Educated somewhere in betweer
university lectures down south, l
compromise by moving to the N
know him well often say that he'ʂ
teaching several years ago, Ferɡ
up the poetry CV; if you want to f
take a trip to fergusthepoet.con
of this book. *Everyone Is Now Unhappy* is his third colle
poetry. He is no longer Worcestershire Poet Laureate, though,
so please stop curtsying.

G000155490

Everyone Is Now Unhappy

Fergus McGonigal

Burning Eye

Burning Eye Books
Never Knowingly
Mainstream

This edition published by Burning Eye Books 2017

www.burningeye.co.uk

@burningeyebooks

Burning Eye Books
15 West Hill, Portishead, BS20 6LG

ISBN 978-1-911570-11-0

For James Green,
in whose company one could never be unhappy.

CONTENTS

ENOUGH

The reader might be bored, or unimpressed,
Or reading this at somebody's behest,
A stranger to the wiles of Mistress Verse,
Whose first response to poetry is terse,
Who fears the shame of not quite understanding,
Who fears that poetry is too demanding,
Yet somehow dull, and lifeless too. They might
(For stranger things have passed) be more than right
To say that poetry's just silly stuff,
To say that ten lines constitutes 'enough'.

DOGS SMARTER THAN CATS

Neighbour says,
'Cats smarter than dogs.'
I raise eyebrow.
Neighbour places
bowl of cat food, bowl of dog food
on one side of garden gate.
Cat jumps over gate,
eats food.
Dog whines.
Neighbour says,
'Cats smarter than dogs.'
I raise both eyebrows,
shrug.
Whatever.

I say,
'Dogs smarter than cats.'
Neighbour laughs.
I place
bowl of cat food, bowl of dog food
on one side of garden gate.
Cat jumps over gate,
lands
on land mine.
Explodes!
Dog stares at sign on gate:
Do not enter – minefield.
'Cats can jump,'
I say,
'but dogs can read.'

BALLADUS POPULUSQUE BANANAS!

I'm going to steal a cake and run away,
    Then hide inside a pot of tea for two,
Where soundly shall I sleep for half a day,
    Allowing me a proper chance to stew,
    Both inside out and through and through and through.
I'll serve myself upon a silver tray,
    In finest Wedgwood china, white and blue.
I've had enough of sensible today.

I'm going to claim to be the letter A,
    I've never liked the prospect of a Q.
I'll always be the first, unlike old J,
    Whose plans to be in front went quite askew –
    The oafish fathead hasn't got a clue –
He goes around pretending to be K,
    When clearly he'd be better off as U!
I've had enough of sensible today.

I'm going to fly a brick without delay
    Before I teach my telephone kung-fu,
Whilst sending all my clothes to Mandalay.
    I wouldn't try this out if I were you –
    You'll end up with extremities of blue.
Instead, consider what I have to say:
    A broken heart is best repaired with glue.
I've had enough of sensible today.

Pants! What now I know is not what once I knew.
    I can't just nonsense everything away.
When all is said, there's little left that's true.
    I've had enough of sensible today.

A LITTLE KNOWLEDGE IS A TEDIOUS THING

There is a certain type of tedious, pedantic nitwit, who, when
   confronted with a wrongly positioned possessive apostrophe,
Will declaim, in loud, dramatic tones designed for all to hear,
   that this is a monumental catostrophe!
Any reasonable person might think that just because one small
   piece is missing from the puzzle of someone else's education,
This isn't necessarily a forewarning of the imminent and total
   collapse of the whole of Western civilisation.
But then, the two phrases 'tedious, pedantic nitwit' and
'reasonable person' are, metaphorically speaking at least, several
   thousand million miles apart,
The phrases not complementing each other like 'fish'
   complements 'chips', 'chinless' complements 'wonder', or
   'that isn't' complements 'art'.

A little later, when peace and calm have returned, you make
   your mind up
To engage in a little pedantic wind-up,
And use the word 'stadiums' in a big, booming voice, loud and
   clear,
So that our tedious, pedantic nitwit could not but hear.

Quick as a flash, the TPN falls into the trap you have set.

'Aah-ahh-aah!
Surely you mean *stadiaaaaaaaaaaaah!*'
To which you casually reply that, being English, and therefore a
   follower of the rules of English grammar, when making a
   singular word plural you usually add an 's',
And that changing the word ending to an 'a' (an 'a', ladies and
   gentlemen? The very thought of it!) to signify a plural
   would create a most hideous syntactic mess.
To which they condescendingly reply, entangling themselves
   further in your trap, that 'Stadium is a Latin word, and one
   should therefore use the Latin plural if one wishes to be
   grammatically proper.'
At which point you apprehend them, like a grammatical copper,
For, you point out, Latin words change their endings not just
   for plurals (*as any fule no*) but also for the nominative,
   vocative, accusative, genitive, ablative and dative,

And this could get really confusing if, every time you wanted
      to use a Latin word, you thought it necessary to speak
      Latin like a Latin native.
The Romans, you point out, really hitting your stride, would
      not have said 'to the stadium' but 'stadio'; neither would
      they have said 'of the stadium' but, instead, 'stadii', so if
      you wish to avoid this semantic and syntactic mess,
Well, then, sssshhhh… about *pluralising* Latin words with an 's'.

Not to be defeated, the nitwit pedant then rails against your
      use of a noun as a verb,
A point which they tragically believe to be intellectually superb.
'*Whom*(!),' they scoff, 'would be such a butcher of the English
      language as to turn a noun into a verb?' and they wait in
      gleeful superiority as if to their brilliant riposte there is no
      reply,
And you say, 'Why,
Surely a certain Mr William Shakespeare was very fond of the
      whole noun-to-verb transformation?'
Highlighting yet another gap in the pedant's education.
(Isn't it a *pity* that such people will not allow us to *pity* them?)

Now, the pedant, if they have any sense,
Will swiftly move to the other side of the pedantic fence
And recant their former pedantry
As a state of mind which is equivalent to being intellectually
      sedentary.
Pedantry, they will have realised (really), is cheap and ineffectual
As a way of trying to *appear* in'ellectual.
The former pedant will hopefully have learned that the answer
      to this question: 'How often is pedantry genuinely clever?'
Is 'Never.'

ALTERNATIVE TITLES FOR THE SCOTTISH PLAY (WHEN YOU ARE PUTTING ON THE SCOTTISH PLAY AND START TO FEEL SLIGHTLY PRETENTIOUS EVERY TIME YOU REFER TO THE SCOTTISH PLAY AS THE SCOTTISH PLAY)

You can call it Macdeath
And refer to Macdeaf,
Or rename it Macjeff,
Or Macbrecht or Macbreath.

You can try out Macteeth,
Or Macboth or Macbeef,
And consider Macdesk,
And allow for Macheath.*

For an apt name, Macbad
Would suffice, like Macmad.
If the lead man is cool,
You could call it Maclad.

If you're rude, use Macbreasts,
If you're risky, Macbet,
If you're clean, use Macbath,
If you're bust, use Macdebt.

But whatever you do,
Upon pain of sure death,
You must never refer
To this play as Macb—

* Blasted, natch.

A DAMNED HEART

after Jam Tart

You're a lost cause, an expensive folly,
You're an awkward pause, you're a dysfunctional trolley,
A wrong turning, a book-burning, a reason for hate,
A hangover, a pile-up, a cracked plate,
A ruptured spleen, a stroppy teen, a broken neck, a scar –
  Each one is what you are.

You're a sick joke, an abomination,
You're a curl of smoke, you're an irritation,
A splitter, a quitter, the final straw,
A misery, a death-trap, tax for the poor,
A crashing plane, unending pain, a streak of piss, it's true –
  Each one of these is you.

You're a super-gun, you're the ammunition,
You're a dying sun, you're a war of attrition,
A drowned sorrow, a no tomorrow, a violent death,
A mindless rant, a war zone, a struggle for breath,
A class-A drug, a killer bug, a solution... in reverse –
  You're all of these and worse.

You're a torn limb, a public hanging,
You're a tale by Grimm, you're a door at night that's banging,
You're Darth Vader, a ram-raider, you're a stain,
The smoking ban, a punch-up, a teacher's cane,
A rusted blade, a bill unpaid, an ego-driven mission –
  You wretched, unelected politician.

A BRIEF LIST, WHICH SHOULD BE SLIGHTLY LONGER, OF THINGS WORTH LIVING FOR

The sound of rain inside a tent,
A cloudless English summer sky,
A promise kept, a letter sent,
And knowing those we hate will die.

The memory of a childhood place,
A lazy morning spent in bed,
A loyal dog, a friendly face,
And laughing when our foes are dead.

The comfort of a favourite book,
The friendships time can never quell,
A gentle breeze, a babbling brook,
And visions of those flames in Hell.

JOSEF VISARIONOVIČ'S FINAL DREAM

I'd started writing a poem about
Josef Stalin's final dream,
having first come up with what I thought was
a half-decent punchline/ending.

I'd picked the metre,
then started on the first few lines,
after which things pretty much ground to a halt.

I hadn't had much sleep the night before,
the osteoarthritis in my left knee
was interfering with the muse,

and my handwriting seemed to be having
a mini mental crisis all of its own.

Instead (although I'd tried and failed
this several times in the past)
I thought I'd try my hand at writing
a poem in the style of Billy Collins:

a personal, but not quite intimate, piece of
chatty, easygoing, narrative, free verse,
whose demotic turn of phrase
would be so lucid

that even an OFSTED inspector
might understand it.

And yes, I did finally get round to writing down
that half-decent punchline/ending, namely:
Josef Stalin dreamt that after his death
they renamed Leningrad 'Lemongrad' in his honour.

TERROR LEMONS (AN EXPLANATION)

Psychotic bastard
and father
of international paranoia
Josef Stalin
grew lemons
throughout
his psychotic bastard life,
neatly exemplifying
that pithy old
slice of wisdom:

*if life gives you lemons,
instigate
a purge of all your enemies.*

NOT ALL THINGS HAPPEN

The moon was not full on that fateless night.
Two would-be lovers missed their only cue,
and pristine sheets remained intact.

No glass was thrown in anger at a wall,
the red wine was not spilled upon the carpet,
and blows were not exchanged.

No feast was held in honour of an honoured guest,
no speech was made, no glasses charged and raised.
Relief's sighed exhalation broke no tension.

Unwritten poems roamed through restless heads,
but found no place to rest upon the page.
Those undiscovered truths lay undiscovered.

INEFFABLE

I sit upon the floor inside
my childhood bedroom, wondering why
it is that God cannot be seen.
'God is in everything,' I'm told,
but I can see this isn't true.

He isn't in my radio.
He isn't in my Action Man.
He isn't in the church on Sunday.
Although I look, I cannot see
him in my mother's vanished face.

I manufacture God from things
left lying on my bedroom floor:
some wooden blocks, a dried-out paintbrush,
the engine from my brother's train set,
and a wig from the dressing-up box.

God balances next to the bookshelf.
'Hello there, God,' I say, but God
does not reply; he doesn't have
a mouth. 'Here, borrow mine,' I say.
I wear God's wig and start to talk.

I talk like God, or how I think
that God would talk. I open-shut
my mouth, then open-shut my mouth
again as silence fills the room.
I stand there, mute, more fish than God.

'For God is very like a fish,'
I say, in pompous, priestly tones.
I open-shut my fish-God mouth
for one last time, de-wig myself,
and put God back inside his boxes.

THE HEROIC WINE-TASTING COMPETITION

The Heroes sat at tables flag-bedecked,
Awaiting starter's orders to get wrecked
On grapes fermented somehow into wine:
The foul, the cheap, the nasty and the fine.
O! What adventures lay in wait that night
For Heroes bold enough to taste the white
And give it marks consistent with its class:
A classic vintage or a load of arse?*
O! These intrepid boozers felt not dread
At guessing if that rather cheeky red
Could grace the table of a lord or duke,
Or if it merely made them want to puke.
These fearless few! This tincture-tasting mob,
The vintners' produce swirling round each gob,
Did set about this monumental quest:
Could quality of wine be rightly guessed?
    They glugged, they gulped, imbibed and some did sup,
To cries of 'Cheers, me dears!' and 'Bottoms up!'
These Heroes faced their labours with no fear,
Some even downing wine as if 'twere beer,
Whilst others drained their glasses drop by drop,
Though none did ever think that they might stop
Their search, as was their holy, blessèd quest:
O! Which wine was the worst and which the best?
And so the Heroes drank and drank some more
As some of them inched closer to the floor,
Whilst, in their quest to guess the bottles' labels,
Some happy few were found beneath the tables.
    By evening's end this bottle-hardened crew,
Convinced the answer to their quest they knew,
Were most sincerely glad they'd come along –
Despite the fact that all of them were wrong!

* Poetic off-licence

ACCENTS

Note to reader: when you come across some italicised words, you have to speak those words in the appropriate accent – in this example, yours.

A friend of mine – who, if I'm brutally honest, cannot really 'do' accents – has claimed to me several times over the years

That when he starts talking to somebody with a different accent, why, he finds himself unconsciously mimicking the accent which he hears.

So, for example, when he recently went to a pub in London and found himself chatting to the barman who was, somewhat inevitably, Australian,

Within ten minutes, he had, apparently, assumed the verbal idiosyncrasies of a fellow Antipodean alien.

Which presumably meant that for the duration of what must have been an increasingly bizarre-sounding conversation,

The aforementioned friend turned every statement into a question by ending each sentence with an ascending interrogative intonation:

Just like this, mate?

While the aforementioned Australian barman probably thought that my friend was... *taking the piss, mate?*

One can't help wondering what would have happened had the Australian barman and my supposedly accentually-mimicking friend

Been joined in their conversation by someone from *Laaaahndon's Eeeeast End.*

Would said friend have assumed the mindset of someone who was becoming accentually confused?

Would he have started speaking *Cock-er-ney to ve Eastendah,* and *Ozzie-rules English to the Australian,* leaving both of his co-conversationalists utterly bemused?

Or, worse still, would he have concocted some form of hybrid Australian/Eastenders *Dick van Dyke/Maiwey Pappins* accent as if he hailed from some hitherto undiscovered nation,

And attempted to converse with these two unfortunate fellows in some *hideously Disneyfied accentual aberration?**

---

* Good luck with working that one out, by the way.

Now, this friend is not alone – quite a few other nincompoops I
    have met over the years have claimed exactly the same
    thing, and seriously expect me to accept that were they to
    converse with, for example, a Scot, *thae would ba turns*
Embark on the conversation with their own unique idiolect,
    and end it speaking in the *manna of a latta-dae Rrrrabbie Burns.*
And, if they were talking to someone who was, let's say, *like,*
    toedally from New York, maaaaan,
That they would, in no time at all, be speaking in the manner
    of a *toedally, like, OMG, dork, maaaaan.*
And am I really supposed to believe that they would abandon
    their *broad Brummie brogue,* or their *reeeally nnnasal*
    Essex tones, or their *Proud! Welsh! Accent!* were they to
    go on holiday to *County Donegal,*
Because within ten minutes of arriving there they would have
    started talking with the cadences of someone whose name
    might be something like – oh, I dunno – *Fergus McGonigal?*
And surely there would be zero chance
Zat zay would, er, start talking like zeeys, when zay were, er,
    speaking to, er, someone from France?
And what are the chances that they would start sounding all
    efficient, organised and maybe just a little bit Teutonic
Ven striking up ze conversation mit sumvunn who vass
    unmistakably Germonic?
And would they become all demonstrably, excessively
    expressive and overemotional *when a-chattin'*
To-a some-a one-a whose-a temperament-a and-a language
    is-a, broadly speaking, a-Latin? (Oh, mamma mia!)
And would they sound like they've been *shmoking too much-sh,*
When shpeaking to shomeone who'sh Dutch-sh?

Well, no – clearly all of this accentual hypothesising is, if you'll
    excuse my French, Italian, German, Irish, American,
    Australian and even English, a big load of crap;
One can't simply turn accents on and off as if one had some
    big, clever accenty tap.
Unless, of course, you're a performance poet, who's written
    and then repeatedly practised a poem containing many
    different accents, all of which he delivered quite
    adequately, if not necessarily masterfully,
Unlike people who claim they mimic accents unconsciously (yeah?
    so how do they know they're doing it?) and successfully,
    but, when they do so, do so, in fact, quite disasterfully.

SEA?

I said the sea was classy
and she said, 'Surely you
mean glassy?' *Glossy sea?*
I said. *You're right; the sea
is glossy more than classy.*
'No – glassy,' she said. 'Glassy.'
You're right, of course, I said.
*It does look grassy green
today.* She gave me quite
a look. 'GLASSY,' she said.
You're right, I said, *it's quite,
quite ghastly; think of all
that sewage for a start.*
'GLAAAAAASSSSSSYYYY,' she said. *The arsey sea?*
I said. She stared at me,
all glassy-eyed, and left.

INZANITY!

Peculiar to witless dullards:
The claim that they are *really mad!*
Or *wild!!* Or, worst of all, they're *zany!!!*

And yet they always dress quite plainly,
Their hair is rarely ever green,
Their words are crass and quite mundane.

If anything, they're far too sane.
Eccentric? Emphatically not.
As edgy as a piece of toast.

It's surely rather dim to boast
That you are something when you're not.
Witless dullards: please take note.

THE SECOND-GREATEST PLEASURE OF BEING A PARENT IS TO SEE OTHER PARENTS PUBLICLY LOSE THE PLOT

You see them out, these over-childrened frights,
Whose squabbling offspring stage such splendid fights.
Stern faces can't hide panic as they shout
Their precious darlings' names out far too loud,
And launch into a brash, alarming volley
Of 'Don't do *that*!' By now, they're off their trolley,
Advancing quite preposterous empty threats.
But children won't be trained like naughty pets
If they can sense their parents lose control.
'Be calm!' you smirk. 'Encourage! Praise! Cajole!'

Envoi
We parents who would offer such advice,
Our memories so vague and imprecise,
So quick to criticise and dish out blame?
They've seen us with our sprogs: we're just the same.

SHALLOW WISDOM

Of the far-too-many things
which grate against my inner peace,
it is the shallow wisdom

of the 'I'm more spiritual than you' brigade
which inspires me, deluded peacenik that I am,
to think thoughts of senseless violence.

Recently, I encountered one such quote,
from a beatified archbishop,
on the mantelpiece of a holiday home.

In blissfully ironic ignorance
of where it was located, this postcard exhorted me:
Aspire not to have more but to be more.

Be more what? Insightful? Wise? Full of bullshit?
It's difficult to know where to begin, really, isn't it?
So let's not even start. No, I jest.

Let's start with a knuckle-duster,
and thwack this sanctimonious little comment
full square in its faux-enlightened face.

'You should aspire to be more quiet,'
I say, above a cacophony of distress,
while lacing up my size ten comment-kicking boots.

Censoredcensoredcensoredcensoredcens
Censoredcensoredcensoredce
Censoredcensoredcensoredcensore

Censoredcensoredcensoredcen
Censoredcensoredcensoredcensoredcensoredcens
Censoredcensoredcensoredcensoredcens

Sensing that my work with this quote
is nearing its conclusion, I douse it with lighter fluid,
flick a match, and stare in holy wonder

at the death dance of its briefly flowering flames.
I walk into the kitchen to make a cup of tea
and notice a quote from the Dalai Lama stuck to the fridge.

DANCES WITH STRANGERS

You walk along an English high street
and dance with the first stranger
who doesn't look deranged.

Their face shows uneasy surprise,
as if you are telling the story of how your garden gate
was once treated for depression with creosote.

You stare at the only patch of blue
in an English sky,
willing it to spread, like a virus which eats grey clouds.

There is no sign of your erstwhile dancing partner.

Apologising to the pavement, you get down on one knee
and propose to a phrase of birdsong
whose reply you cannot decipher.

You dance with all the mad thoughts in your head
until their feet ache.
You dance and you dance and you dance
in case the music is still playing.

TIME AND SEASON

Time meets with Season every Tuesday
to talk about philosophy
and poetry and opera,
but Season only wants to talk
about celebrities and pop
music and *Coronation Street*.

'Although I like the lucid insights
of Bertrand Russell, nothing equals
the wisdom shown by Seneca…'
Season confuses Bertrand Russell
with Russell Brand; the conversation
takes some unexpected detours.

'I swoon for Byron, Keats and Shelley.
Romantic poets represent
humanity's apotheosis…'
Season expresses admiration
for Ronan Keating's amorous
endeavours, and his back catalogue.

'Where Mozart's operas play to full
houses, enlightenment can dazzle
even the laggard's loutish heart…'
Season says Moz's favourite soap
opera was *Coronation Street*,
'Which shows he had at least some taste.'

Time is in love with Season's presence.
Season is not aware of Time's
affections. Time understands this.

A PREDICTION

When I am old, I will degenerate.
My joints will moan and grate, and getting out
of bed will be a trial. All those years
of healthy eating, going to the pool,
and cycling to work: all will have been
in vain. You can't hold back the foetid tide
of geriatric decay. Sixty isn't
the new forty, despite the narcissistic
delusions harboured by arse-brained journalists.
Mealtimes will be a bowl of pills: there won't
be room for any real food. The day's
greatest adventure? Making it as far as
the television room, where, slumped in front
of Netflix, sleep will interrupt the narratives.
The melancholy strains of afternoon
will kill my spirit further, when I see
that yet another day has somehow slipped my
grasp. I'll wonder how I ever got so old
so fast. The night will bring its old regrets,
and sleep will be my practice for the grave.
Did someone call my name? No? Never mind.
When I am old, I will die...

NICE TRY

Nobody told us anything useful. Those with influence and a weak grasp of semantics endlessly fashioned statements from car-crash ideas. Meanwhile, everyone watched TV.

Nobody told us that things would get worse before they got even worse. Those with influence cultivated shrines to their own vanity. Meanwhile, everyone ate far, far too much.

Nobody told us how to write a poem. Those with influence promoted this ignorance. Meanwhile, everyone got off on their own brand of computer-generated violence.

Nobody told us where to find Jesus on a Tuesday afternoon. Those with influence secretly doubted the existence of Tuesdays. Meanwhile, everyone forgot the words to their favourite Easter egg.

Nobody told us about the deliciousness of mediocre supermarket ready meals. Those with influence pretended to chop the vegetables. Meanwhile, everyone dined on horsemeat surprise.

Nobody told us how to erase a past. Those with influence placed gold coins on the eyelids of their deceased indiscretions. Meanwhile, everyone bypassed the super-injunction by storming Twitter with pitchforks and moral outrage.

Nobody told us that the Queen's garden parties included a section for naturists. Those with influence left their invitations on the mantelpiece to impress the visitors. Meanwhile, everyone bought corgi-flavoured lollipops from the overpriced gifte shoppe.

Nobody told us because nobody knew. Those with influence wasted their entire lives in the futile pursuit of holding on to their influence. Meanwhile, everyone went back to watching TV.

PRELUDE, OP. 1914, NO. 1

The Prelude opens with a chord
Whose barbed-wire notes are grimly scored
And from whose depths a melody is born,
A tune to make both Youth and Old Age mourn.
With bugle, fife and drum,
It tells us what's to come.
Disharmony and tune compete:
Advance-withdraw; attack-retreat.
No cheerful *leitmotifs* for those who wait,
But gas attacks and bayonets and hate.

A shrill, forbidding choir joins in,
And sings of shells, and next-of-kin,
And life amid the ruins of despair,
Where shrapnel-shaped crescendos fill the air.
A military beat,
From tired, arrhythmic feet,
Is tapped like Morse code with no scheme,
And warns that things aren't what they seem.
The Prelude plays the coda's closing phrase,
And rumour speaks of dark, demented days.

As Youth prepares to be betrayed,
The Prelude's final chord is played:
Off-key, off-beat, and fading far too fast.
This Prelude to the War could never last.
Its tense, unquiet calm
Was simply War's alarm,
Which woke up Albion, who found
Vast armies with no common ground
Prepare to fight, whilst trying to ignore
What really happens when we go to war.

GENERATION GAP

There will be rust and bricks for all.
All art will cease to matter.
Taking offence will be a virtue.
We'll stand beside the smashed glass front
of England's last remaining high street shop
and smile like idiots whose senseless adoration of the ego
is captured in an endless rash of selfies.
Of course I'd love to see another photo of
you looking studied, you fascinating child.

There will be bones and phlegm for all.
The virtue of the stupid
will be the latest must-have fashion item.
Love will be redacted from all novels, plays and poems,
and nobody will notice.
We'll paint this land with blood and concrete,
half-sing its national anthem
with flecks of spit, sandpapered fists, and bloodshot eyes.
As eloquent as, like, whatever.

There will be petty cash and canned laughter for all.
Monochrome will be the new black.
Lack of self-awareness will be the new black.
And while we wait,
the ironed-on expressions of the surgically enhanced
will provide a message for the world,
for those who care to read it.
Our best intentions will mean nothing in the end.
That wasn't it.

IN THE CULTURAL BARGAIN BIN TODAY, WE HAVE

after Byron Vincent

Life deodorant,
Not the truth,
Simon Cowell's
Cloven hoof.

Books about
Some tragic life,
Last week's girlfriend/
Next week's wife.

Racist jokes
From ITV
(Autumn nineteen
eighty-three).

Pirate-copied
Barbie dolls,
Fatalistic
Exit polls.

Teenage games
Of Truth or Dare,
Elton John's
Bionic hair.

Shark-infested
Legal teams,
This week's nightmares/
Last week's dreams.

Answers from
The Great Beyond,
Harry Potter's
Flaccid wand.

All the tat
You'll never need,
Last year's savings/
This week's greed.

Cauterised
Aesthetic taste?
Welcome to
The Human Waste.

ICE CREAM BLUES

*'I don't eat ice cream. It's something to do with being
straight. Ice cream is a bit... you know...'*

Richard Hammond

'...hahaha... ice cream... hahahaha... you know...'

The Audience

What massed inadequates are these? What fools
whose foul, unlettered laughter spills like shit
from foetid mouths and vicious hearts? They are
not men, but weaklings all: too delicate
from fear of sexuality not theirs
to feel the brutal damage which they cause.
    How fitting that such lame unsavouries
should take their drooping cue from one who is
so pusillanimous he fears to eat
an ice cream on a stick. But what's to fear
from mere confection? What's to fear when all
that's there is nothing more than ice cream on
a stick? What's seen depends upon the man
who sees: he sees the thing he wants to see,
and thus reveals himself. And this man sees
no harmless, childish ice cream on a stick:
he sees a large, intimidating cock.
His masculinity under attack –
from whom? Himself, of course; *his* mind; *his* thoughts –
he cannot shake this phallic vision from
his troubled, scared imagination. Look!
For now the ice cream in his mind is oozing
its sticky cream all down his manly hand.
'Out! Out! Damned spot!' But from where? And as what?

BANALITY

You want to pulverise a bag
of Walkers cheese and onion crisps
with your bare fists, shouting, 'Take that!
You bastard cheese and onion bastards!'

The first blow proves to be decisive:
the bag explodes at either end.
The crisp diaspora has spread
too far. This isn't good enough.

You'd only got as far as '...*that*!'
You find the packing tape, repair
the bag, replace the crisps, then wind
the tape around the bag some more.

The second, third, fourth, and fifth blows
prove far more satisfactory.
The strengthened bag's resilience
impresses you. You get a hammer.

Not wanting to destroy your kitchen,
you take your bag of crisps outside
and place them on a Black & Decker
Workmate, where they await destruction.

You hammer crisps and swear out loud
all afternoon till all that's left
is your undoubted mastery
over a bag of Walkers crisps.

UP DOWN

The existential bicycle decides
he needs a holiday and takes himself
to Holland where the horizontality
impresses greatly. Not since Norfolk has
the bicycle been treated to such flatness.
    The existential bicycle believes
there must be more to life than ups and downs.
The holiday on Holland's flats has left
the existential bicycle believing
that 'more to life' exists upon those flats
and not the endless ups and downs of old.
    The existential bicycle appears
to Jesus in a dream. 'Take up your wheels
and spin!' commands the Bearded-Sandalled One.
The existential bicycle exists
beyond *The Dream of Jesus and the Bike.*
The existential bicycle rides up
and down and dreams of being on the flats.
    The existential bicycle defies
the laws of gravity. He floats as if
he is in space or on the surface of
the Moon. The music in the background waits,
and leaves the existential bicycle
to wonder briefly when he will wake up.
    The existential bicycle traverses
the U-shaped valley. He consents to having
his photo taken for an article
about the joys of mountain biking in
the Peak District, despite the fact that he
is not a mountain bike and finds no joy
in mountain biking. Checking on his satnav,
the existential bicycle discovers
that Wales is not a part of the Peak District.
He leans against a chapel wall and wonders
why he no longer finds the landscape awe-
inspiring. All he thinks of now is Holland,
and how it is that existential bikes
appear to lack free will. *I'm sick of hills,*
he thinks, and starts to climb another hill.

The existential bicycle is more
than lost; he doesn't even know the road
he took to get there. *There*, wherever that
might be. He searches for a road to take
him back. Remembering that old phrase *All
roads lead to Rome*, he wonders if the same
applies to *All roads lead back home*. He takes
the nearest road and travels, more in hope
than expectation, as a thought reminds
him that he either has no home or does
not know its whereabouts. But off he pedals.

The existential bicycle is in
Brazil! Completely unaware of all
the football, he is more spectacularly
off-track than ever. Following the crowd,
he finds himself inside a football ground.
The bicycle dissimulates his lack
of football nous by donning a Brazil shirt.
After a grim game during which Brazil
achieve a victory combining skill,
weird serendipity and a catalogue
of quite implausible decisions from
the Portuguese officials, Bicycle
throws off his shirt to reveal a Biblical
quotation, then he does a giant wheelie
along a crowded boulevard before
collapsing in a heap outside a bar.

A LETTER TO BEAUTY

Dear Beauty,
    If you dressed in a mouldy potato sack
With mud on the front and stains on the back,
Then ran twenty times round an athletics track,
If you looked like the survivor of a nuclear attack:
You'd still be a world-class cutie,
My pricelessly rare, occasionally bare,
Though not-quite-yet-antique Beauty.

If your hair disappeared, and your teeth all fell out,
If you drank too much beer, then grew fat and got gout,
So that when people saw you, they'd say, 'She's *well* stout!'
And you swore all the time like some tedious lout:
I'd be there every day, out of love, and not duty;
I'd stay by your side, until one of us died,
For deep down, you'd still be a beauty.

If you ever went out to the Old Wild West
But forget to pack up your bulletproof vest,
Then got into trouble, resisted arrest,
Broke out of jail, just after you'd 'fessed:
When the sheriff and his men got all shooty,
I'd pull a neat stunt, and jump right in front
Of the bullets to safeguard your beauty.

If you lost every ounce of both culture and learning
And gave up on smiling whilst taking up gurning,
If you thought that you'd spend twice as much as I'm earning:
You'd still be *bellissimo con multo-frutti*,
You'd still beat the highlights from *Così fan tutte*,
You marvellous creature, I'd still wanna eat yer!
For you are a wondrous beauty.

Now, if you get old and forget who I am,
Remember, instead, what I've said at this slam:
There's no one for whom I give more of a damn
Than you, my dear Beauty, my darling, my Gem.

Yours truly,
The Beast (aka Fergus M)

NEWCASTLE! *NEWCASTLE!*

'Newcastle!' comes the strangled squawk of horror.
'It's said Newcastle!' *Not where I come from,*
I say (the posh-voiced, prosperous southerners
from Royal Tunbridge Wells pronounce the word
according to their RP accent).
'The word's pronounced Newcastle!' *Not by me,*
I say. 'But that is how you're supposed to say it:
Newcastle!' *Yes,* I say, *as long as you're
a northerner; were I to say* Newcastle
*amid my plummy, elongated vowels I'd sound
very pretentious. Furthermore, I don't
insist on you pronouncing Tunbridge Wells
as Tunbridge Wells and not* Tunbridge Wells. 'Well, in
an ideal world,' he says, 'you'd say Newcastle.'
In an ideal world, I say, *our accents wouldn't matter.*

WHAT'S IN A BIRD?

after Billy Collins

The birds had had enough of singing
about their territorial
disputes; they yearned to write their thoughts.

After the snow which fell one night,
a sheet of white stretched out across
the surface of the silent garden.

A robin broke the stillness with
a carefully constructed haiku
about the suffering of robins.

A sparrow wrote a manifesto
entitled *Death to All the Cats*;
a chaffinch offered her critique.

A thrush composed some smutty jokes
on nominative determinism
and signed off with *I'm here all week.*

The rain soon fell and covered all
their little works with wet full-stops,
the fate which will befall all writing.

THE TRUTH ABOUT LOVE

after Auden

Some say that love is all you need,
    And some say it's a drug,
Some say that love's a dirty deed,
    And some say it's a bug,
But when I started looking for it,
    And coyly asked around,
Most people told me to ignore it,
    Or said, 'It can't found!'

Does it hide in the dark like a virus,
    Which mutates far too fast for a cure?
Is it written on ancient papyrus?
    Is it too much for us to endure?
Does it torture the souls of all madmen?
    Is it sent from below or above?
Is it sold by unscrupulous admen?
    Just what is the truth about love?

I've read about it many times,
    In florid prose and verse,
I've heard about its torrid crimes,
    I've heard that it's a curse.
It seems to me it's everywhere,
    But largely undiscovered,
I've heard that when it brings despair,
    Your soul can't be recovered.

Does it wear too much make-up or blusher?
    Is its hair done by Vidal Sassoon?
Has it ever set foot inside Russia?
    Does it like to stare up at the moon?
Does it stand around nervously waiting?
    Does it need an encouraging shove?
Does it have an opinion on dating?
    Just what is the truth about love?

I searched beneath the kitchen sink,
    I peered above the loo,
I sat and had a good old think,
    But didn't have a clue.
I glanced across towards the door,
    I peeped upon a shelf,
Then sat upon the bedroom floor,
    And looked inside myself.

Does it like to behave like a moron?
    Can it ever admit when it's wrong?
Does it cry when it knows there's a war on?
    Is its nose just a little too long?
Is it likely to get too excited,
    When it finds a lost favourite glove?
Does it struggle with being short-sighted?
    Just what is the truth about love?

Now, just before I turn and go,
    There's something I should say.
This 'love' is something that I know;
    I've led you all astray.
I know that love's no abstract word,
    Elusive, never found.
To say so would be quite absurd,
    For love is all around.

It's the son who has slept on my shoulder,
    It's the hug which I give to a friend,
It's the, 'Hey, look! We're thirty years older!'
    It's the walking with you to the end.
It's the story we'll never stop writing,
    It's the sadness our time's not enough,
And it's you, 'cause you're bloody exciting.
    There you have it: the truth about love.

NOCTURNE

Tonight, before you fall asleep, if
you grasp an ink pen in your hands, will words
be written on the sheet when you awake?

Will lines appear across the surface of
the wooden floor, the wall, the bedroom ceiling,
explaining how you made it through the night?

Or will you write a poem on her body,
of beauty, happiness, and love-that-is,
to be washed off in the morning's rain?

BORN MIDDLE-AGED

While most children spend most of their childhoods (the
    waking part) variously complaining that something isn't fair,
    fighting with siblings, shouting at parents, and generally
    making their way towards being enraged,
By contrast, I had a brother who was born middle-aged.
Now, no doubt some of you might start thinking, *Oh, I had a*
    cousin like that; we used to call him Captain Sensible,
But I would have to stop you right there, for the level of juvenile
    midlife behaviour displayed by my brother was incomparable
    (as well as being utterly incomprehensible).

For example, once, when I tried to goad him into a full-on
    dramatic and infantile retaliation,
He simply reminded me of his solicitor's most recent legal
    communication.
'The key phrase,' he said, barely looking up from his *Times*
    crossword, 'starts with the word *restraining*…
Now, enough of your foolish and puerile feigning,
Run along while I solve seven down:
Synonymous with younger brother, five letters – *clown*.'

For his sixth birthday, I rashly bought him a cute, cuddly teddy.
He just looked at me wearily, sighed, took his glasses off, rubbed
    his eyes, and said, 'What? That time of year already?'
The thing is, because he liked things to be 'really straight',
His transitional object to date
Had been a set square,
And I had naively thought that a teddy bear
Might be more suitable.
He unwrapped it and then sat there, his expression inscrutable.
'I'm sure it'll be very useful and it is just what I have always wanted,'
He eventually said, before placing it in the wastepaper basket.

My brother's middle-aged childhood seemed to be an endless
    merry-go-round of
Advising Father about his pension,
Taking inhibitors for his hypertension,
Talking to 'young people' with complete condescension,
Spending Saturday afternoons cleaning the car,
Being snooty about music with 'the electric guitar',

Writing letters to the local journal
In the hectoring tones of a retired colonel,
Using words like *preposterous* and *infernal*,
Insisting his milk be at least semi-skimmed,
Keeping the edges of the lawn neatly trimmed,
And his favourite treat:
Pruning the wisteria while listening to *The Archers*' Omnibus
    Edition.

You're probably expecting me to say, 'And then came the
    midlife crisis, which turned out to be adolescence, after
    which he started hanging out with other teens;
He even started experimenting, with the *idea* of wearing jeans.'
But my brother wasn't cut out to be that unconventional;
He stayed middle-aged and continued to view us childish
    children as dim and one-dimensional.

I think it must have been a really tough gig, being naturally
    self-disciplined, when all the other children were naturally
    self-naughty,
Adults always saying that you're seven, going on forty,
And years later, when everyone's forgotten,
Along comes a younger brother with some wholly misbegotten
Poem... reminding everyone.
I fully expect the last laugh to belong to my sensible sibling:
While we enjoy our 'second childhood', all senile and dribbling,
He'll be gleefully running around, experiencing the newfound
    freedoms...
                ...of his first childhood.

HOTHOUSING IDIOTS

You can ban television until they leave home,
　　You can set them assignments, both written and read,
You can take them on cultural visits to Rome,
　　And cram lots of arcane facts into each head,
　　Profound and obscure, from A through to Z.
But something you shouldn't attempt, even once,
Is this sort of stuff with a child who's a dunce.

You can make them learn violin, piano, bassoon,
　　The harpsichord, clarinet, organ and flute,
Insist that they know every classical tune:
　　Each plucked pizzicato, each whistling toot,
　　Each oompah-pah, cowbell, and honkety-hoot!
But, really, you shouldn't attempt all this lot
With a child who is clearly a bit of a clot.

You can make them learn Latin and Greek *'for a laugh'*,
　　Make linear equations *'a rare, special treat'*.
For *'fun'* they can symbolise π on a graph,
　　While *'break time'* means *'work which you have to repeat'*,
　　As you turn up the dial which is marked *'hothouse heat'*.
But I wouldn't expect any scholarly wins
From a child who will one day be emptying bins.

You may showcase your offspring with no self-awareness,
　　We'll sit there eyes glazed and quite unimpressed,
For stealing a childhood's the height of unfairness;
　　Already we see that they're properly stressed,
　　Neurotically blinking and likely depressed.
And I wouldn't expect any filial love
From a child who's been ruined by all the above.

AND STILL THEY DIDN'T SACK ME

i.m. Sports Day commentary, 2009

The drama teacher's pissed again,
The drama teacher's pissed.
He's sounding absurd
As he slurs every word.
I think that perhaps his vision is blurred.
It's a sight to behold and not to be missed
When the drama teacher gets thoroughly pissed.

The man with the mic has had one too many,
He's had one too many, I fear.
What's he thinking
By drinking and drinking?
Look at his reputation sinking
In cider and whisky and champagne and beer.
He's had one too many, I fear.

The Year 4 tutor is staggering home,
Staggering, rollicking drunk.
Will his drunken gob
Lose him his job?
Reeling and stumbling like an artless slob,
A reckless old fool, a bum and a punk,
He's staggering, rollicking drunk.

HALF A POEM

The glass half-empty
or the work half-done.
What good is a half
    to anyone?

A dish half-washed
or a house half-built?
A song half-sung
    or half a kilt?

Half a TV
or half a book?
Half a policeman
    catching half a crook?

Half a person
living half a life?
Half of a husband
    marrying half a wife?

Half a solution
to half a puzzle?
Half a dog
    with half a muzzle?

Half of my shoes:
the left half, of course.
Half of a bet
    on half of a horse?

Half of a mirror
for half of your head?
Half of some bling
    for half street-cred?

Half an exam
or half a play?
Half a teapot
    on half a tray?

Half of a wedding
or half a divorce?
Half persuasion,
    half brute force?

I think a half
is a useless part.
That's why I gave you
    all of my heart.

FATHER CHRISTMAS IS REAL

for Fintan, Conor, Declan, Myles and Aidan

My sons were always totally dismissive
Of sitting down to write a yuletide missive,
Addressed to some red-coated, bearded fraud,
Who still delivered presents when ignored.
They thus arrived at this robust conclusion:
Belief in Father Christmas was delusion.

And so, each year, with silent steps I'd creep,
And place on beds of children not asleep
Those bulging stockings full of Christmas tat,
Then make a large disturbance. What. A. Prat.
And as they lay awake inside their beds,
This thought went running through their little heads:
This Father Christmas chap was just their dad,
A role at which he was uniquely bad.

But now they're old enough to learn this fact:
The clumsy Father Christmas was an act.
Throughout their growing up I did conceal
The truth that Father Christmas is quite real,
But wouldn't visit here to fill one stocking,
Because their bad behaviour was so shocking.

This truth may come to them as some surprise
And make them less the cynic and more wise.
I know they'll probably find it quite unnerving
To learn they were completely undeserving
Of all that jolly childish festive stuff.
(Let's hope they don't now storm off in a huff.)

WHAT COULD BE MORE CHARMING THAN WATCHING OTHER PEOPLE'S CHILDREN PERFORMING MUSIC ON A STAGE?

They stand there looking not-so-cute,
With violin, trumpet, sax or flute.
The instruments, some flat, some sharp,
Go screech and scrape and scratch and *parp!*

They sing some bloody awful song,
Whose melody they get quite wrong.
Then yet another tune is fumbled,
The words are garbled, mangled, mumbled.

You read the programme notes anew
And learn you're only halfway through
This soul-destroying sonic traffic;
Thoughts of escape become quite graphic.

You want to stand and scream and shout,
'O, please, dear God! Please, let me out!'
But don't. Instead, your teeth start grinding,
The tension in you slowly winding.

That's it! you think. *I'm leaving now!*
Just as the children start to bow.
You clap so loud your hands start stinging,
And thank the Lord for no more singing.

PLAY NICELY

What the world's warring
nations need
is a no-nonsense
mum,
a modern mitochondrial matriarchal
Eve
reminding us we're all
quite closely
connected cousins.
'Play nicely,'
she would command,
treating us like
the tyrannical brats
that
we are.

Before we got
to fighting,
she would sit us down
with a chocolate cake
in the shape
of our countries:
united.
'You want borders?'
she would ask,
as she held out
a knife,
for one of us
to grasp.
'One cuts,
the other chooses.'

Do it mum's way;
that way,
nobody
loses.

HOW TO ESTABLISH LASTING WORLD PEACE

People who listen to Johnny Marr
while driving
are three times more likely to
cede right of way,
acknowledge thanks,
smile,
wave,
stay awake on tedious journeys.

People who listen to Johnny Marr
while gardening
are seven times less likely to
be stung by a wasp,
cut a worm in half,
decapitate daffodils,
ignore the hosepipe ban,
kidnap the next-door neighbour's cat.

People who listen to Johnny Marr
while planning the end of the world
are almost certain to
experience an epiphany during track 6,
pick up a guitar,
fail to work out the guitar part for track 6,
forget what they were doing,
establish lasting world peace instead.

ASTRONAUT HAT

for Jon and Rupert

While other boys played Cops and Robbers,
our gang played games of Good Cop/Bad Cop,
which does create some limits when
there are only of three of you to start with.

My turn for Bad Cop came around.
I dragged my Joint Best Friend inside
on yet another trumped-up charge:
possession of a younger sister.

'I haven't got a younger sister,'
he huffed, convincingly indignant.
'Really?!' I hollered in his face,
then pistol-whipped him with a cap gun.

This compromised his space helmet
(we often played in outer space),
and Joint Best Friend collapsed on to
the floor in gasping, choking breaths.

Enter Good Cop, smoking a pencil,
a *Jackie* yearbook in his hand.
'I like the picture of your sister
on page eleven. Very glam.'

'Really?' said Joint Best Friend. 'Let's see!'
but Good Cop passed the book to me,
already opened at the page.
'They could be twins,' I said, and laughed.

'Admit your guilt, we'll let you walk,'
said Good Cop as I aimed the cap gun
at Joint Best Friend's head.
'Or not,' I sneered, and pulled the trigger.

'Nice work,' said Good Cop as we cleaned
no brains off the page, revealing
the picture of a sparkly hairbrush,
completely FREE to every new subscriber!!!

THIS MUCH

after Nash

More than a prisoner hates his cell,
More than a bully likes to shove
Or the hypochondriac hates to be well,
That's how much you I love.

I love you more than a dog can bark,
More than a cloud holds rain.
I love you more than the moon lights the dark,
And more than work is a pain.

As a bad comedian likes his jokes,
Or the sky likes to be blue,
As a bicycle wheel needs its spokes,
That's how much I love you.

I love you more than a bird can sing,
And more than our car won't start.
I love you as much as a wedding needs a ring,
And more than a horse pulls a cart.

I swear to you by the world at large,
For everyone to see,
As a sensible soldier hates the word 'Charge!'
That's how you're loved by me.

TOWARDS THE LAKE

Blank canvas sky is painted summer blue,
with puffs and wisps of whitened grey which lend
authentic Englishness and give the land
a shadowed green. I notice, just below

this sleeping, mile-long, dusty, stone-strewn track,
an arc of blossomed trees, a pink-stained shield
which hides the lake, to let it stay unveiled
until I reach the end of my brief trek.

And as I walk beside this field, this hedge,
these breeze-carried butterflies, this closed gate,
this flock of off-white sheep, I look right out
at everything on view from this high ridge,

and wonder: if this world were now a poem –
and not substantive, concrete, or molecular;
where fields and trees and all were metaphors,
all rhyming according to nature's whim –

how new and vast and strange these things would look,
with every colour singing, every sound
a dancing pattern. Alive, here I stand
and watch this poem stretch towards the lake.

NOW WE ARE TEN

Two people stand outside the train.
They wave goodbye. They wave again.
They wave once more. They call a loud,
'Goodbye!' They walk towards a crowd
Of other parents who, today,
Are sending children far away.
Departure brings a separation
From childhood left at King's Cross Station.

HOW WE ARE REMEMBERED

A black-haired lad with freckles, only ten,
was walking on the pavement. As I left
the newsagent's, I saw him take a step,
without a backwards glance, into the path
of moving traffic. Odd how careless youth
can be. I knew that lad back then: a child
I taught at school. And now I see him, once
again, his body flying through the air,
a picture in my mind, no more; I hear
no sound, but merely see his arms and legs
mid-flail, suspended six feet up, moments
before he landed with a thud. I called
his name and ran across the road, the cars
no longer moving. Carl, no longer moving.
He'd fallen in a heap. I called his name.

     I held the flowers in my hand, a bright
and cheerful bunch. I wondered: *Should I buy
these from the Co-op?* Knowing – *Yes, of course,
a rushing man will only buy his flowers
from such a place as this.* And then I saw
a black-haired girl with freckles, twelve years on.
Her brother Carl had fallen in a heap.
In an instant, we caught each other's eye.
A silent moment, hesitating. Pause.
Another second calculating. Strange
how quick the brain can be, to see
a face from all those years ago and know
it was his sister's, thinking what to say beyond
Hello. She beat me to the thought and spoke,
with smiling mouth and quiet eyes. 'Hello?
Weren't you that teacher who was there with Carl?'

LISTEN

Do not accept the things I say,
like, 'Every picture speaks a thousand words,
yet poems paint a thousand pictures,'
because, although it sounds profound,
it isn't. Poems are not pictures.
They are. Don't listen to a word I say.

Poems are shooting stars; we miss them
unless we keep our eyes wide open.
So read. Pick up a book of poems,
or else you'll miss those miracles of light.
Don't listen. Poems are just words,
and shooting stars aren't even stars.

Like truth, a poem's best discovered.
Oh, sure, occasionally we stumble
upon such things we think insightful,
but usually that's when we're pissed.
When last night's revelations reach
the light of day, they hide their faces.
No need to search for truth: it's everywhere.

Things are, and they are not. A poem is,
and also isn't. Hold those thoughts.
Don't hold those thoughts. But find your truth.
And be alive to shooting stars.
Bottom line? Work it out yourself.
And sometimes, never, always, often,
maybe, who knows? Listen. To a poet.

EVERYONE IS NOW UNHAPPY

Epitaph on a year.

The sun will shine again –
The clouds will clear.
The birds will sing –
And flowers will appear.

ACKNOWLEDGEMENTS

Many thanks to Brenda Read-Brown for the gigs, Maggie Doyle for the constant encouragement and support, Harriet Evans for her amazing powers of perception, Clive Birnie and Jenn Hart at Burning Eye for making it all happen, and Gemma and the boys for their unwavering love.